CORNERSTONES
for
Writing

Pupil's Book
Year 5

**Alison Green, Jill Hurlstone
and Diane Skipper**

Series Editor
Jean Glasberg

CAMBRIDGE
UNIVERSITY PRESS

Five steps to

GOOD WRITING

1 **Modelling:** use a model text to help you learn how to write your own text

Use the activities in this book

2 **Plan your own text**

Use the planning frames or the activities in this book

3 **Draft your text**

Work on your own text

4 **Revise and edit your text**

Work on your own text

5 **Publish your text**

Work on your own text

 When you see this symbol, do this activity with a partner or in a group.

CONTENTS

How to write
a playscript

1 How a play is organised

1 Use **copymaster** 1.

2 Use **copymaster** 2. Use this word bank to help you.

<u>Verbs</u>

Speech	Action
say	walk
shout	cuddle
whisper	sit
demand	enter
cry	exit
groan	stand
plead	rush
laugh	look

<u>Adverbs</u>

happily	furiously
angrily	slowly
crossly	quickly
shyly	menacingly
sadly	greedily
fiercely	loudly
soothingly	sarcastically

3 Read this passage from *Crummy Mummy and Me* by Anne Fine.

Write it as a playscript. Include stage directions and dialogue.

Act it out with a partner.

Minna wakes up one morning feeling ill. Instead of sympathy, her mum tells her:

"You don't *look* very poorly."

That's what she said. And she said it suspiciously, too, as if I was one of those people who's always making excuses to stay off school.

"Well, I feel absolutely rotten."

"You don't look it."

"I'm sorry!" I snapped. (I was getting pretty cross.) "Sorry I can't manage a bright-green face for you! Or purple spots on my belly! Or all my hair falling out! But I feel rotten just the same!"

And I burst into tears.

(Now that's not like me.)

"Now that's not like you," said Mum, sounding sympathetic at last. "You must be a little bit off today."

"I am not *off*," I snarled through my tears. "I'm not leftover milk. Or rotten fish."

"There, there," Mum soothed. "Don't fret, Minna. Don't get upset. You just hop straight back up those stairs like a good poppet, and in a minute I'll bring you something nice up on a tray."

That was a bit more like it, as I think you'll agree. So I stopped snivelling and went back to bed.

From Crummy Mummy and Me by Anne Fine

Read the story of 'Tommy and the Ghost'. Write it as a playscript.

Put in action and speech stage directions.

Use the word bank on page 4 to help you.

Rehearse the scene with your partner.

"Are you sure you'll be all right?" asked the owner of the haunted house.

"I know what to do," said Tommy. "You just leave me to it."

"Well, make yourself at home!" said the owner.

That's what Tommy did. As soon as the owner had gone, he stretched out in front of the fire, and finished off the owner's bottle of best brandy.

Just on midnight – the clock in the hall was still striking – there was a kind of rustle. And there was the ghost! Standing right in front of Tommy.

"Hello!" the ghost whispered.

"Hello to you!" said Tommy.

"Well, Tommy, how are you doing?"

"I can't complain," said Tommy. "But how do you know my name?"

"Easy," whispered the ghost. "I know names."

"How did you get in here?" Tommy asked. "Not through that door. I was watching."

"Through the keyhole."

"Stuff!" said Tommy. "I don't believe you."

"But I did," whispered the ghost.

"Nonsense!" said Tommy. "You're too large by half. What next? I suppose you'll tell me that you can get through the neck of a bottle?"

"I can and all," whispered the ghost.

"Never," said Tommy.

"I can then."

"Prove it!"

"Look," whispered the ghost. "Can't you believe your own eyes, Tommy?"

And with that, the ghost drew itself up, and then drew itself down into the brandy bottle.

At once Tommy put the cork back into the top of the bottle. He went straight out of the house and down to the river and threw the bottle, plunk, under the middle arch.

"You drank all my best brandy!" exclaimed the owner of the house.

"Fair exchange," said Tommy. "This house of yours will never be haunted again."

'Tommy and the Ghost' by Kevin Crossley-Holland

1 Read the character profiles of Mum, Minna, Crusher and Gran.

Then read the dialogue and decide who says each line.

Write the answers in your book. Give a reason for your choice.

Name: Gran
Age: 59
Appearance: sensible clothes, light blue hair
Personality: kind, determined, easily upset. Hates Mum's appearance

Name: Minna
Age: 9
Appearance: neat and tidy. Sensible clothes
Personality: organised, sensible. Thinks like an adult

Name: Mum
Age: 30
Appearance: punk
Personality: untidy, caring, unconventional. A good mother, but sometimes lazy

Name: Crusher
Age: 29
Appearance: punk
Personality: kind, caring, lazy. Can be impatient

1 "Wotcha Granny... I hope one of those plates you're rinsing is for me."

2 "A girl's hair is supposed to be her crowning glory! Royal blue hair! Royal blue hair! What will the neighbours think? Answer me that!"

3 "I want to go down to the launderette after tea. I'm out of socks."

4 "Crusher, fancy a game of cards?"

5 "You go straight to bed. I'll take care of you. You tuck yourself up comfortably, and I'll bring up something nice on a tray."

6 "You've got your feet well and truly under the table, haven't you, young Maggot?"

7 "If I find out who it was, I'll rip his ears off!"

8 "Oh, you're getting older all the time. You don't need that much sleep."

2 Use **copymaster 3**.

3 Read this passage about Minna's gran.

> I like my gran. She lives right on the other side of the estate, but she comes over almost every tea-time. She picks Miranda out of the cot, and coos to her, and then she sits with Miranda on her knee on the only bit of sofa that isn't leaking stuffing. Mostly, she tells Mum off. She says now Mum's a mother of two, it's time she grew up and pulled herself together. She tells Mum she should throw all her safety-pin earrings and fishnet tights into the dustbin, and go out and buy herself a nice, decent frock from Marks and Spencers.

From Crummy Mummy and Me by Anne Fine

Write a character profile for Gran. Use the picture to help you. Set it out like this:

Name: ....
Age: ....
Appearance: ....
Personality: ....

4 One day Mum dyes her hair bright blue.
With a partner, act out the scene when Gran sees Mum's hair for the first time.

Think about:

> What will my character say?
>
> What will my character do?
>
> How will my character react to the other character in the scene?

Now write the scene as a play. Include stage directions.

Does the dialogue reflect your character's personality?

Read the character profiles for these two characters.
Think of some more details to add in your book.

Name:	Edward
Age:	71
Appearance:	smart, always wears a shirt and tie
Personality:	kind, fun-loving, likes going out, lonely

Name:	Niraj
Age:	8
Appearance:	casual clothes
Personality:	friendly, inquisitive, mischievous

With a partner, act out a scene between these characters.

Think about these questions:

- Have they just met, or do they know each other?

- What are they talking about? (e.g. their families? football?)

- What do they say which reveals something about their characters?

- Does something else happen in the scene before or after this conversation?

Write the scene as a playscript.
Act it out with your partner using the script.
Does the dialogue reflect your character's personality?

Choose one of these characters.

Make sure you choose a different one from your partner!

Write a profile of your character like this:

Name:	
Age:	
Appearance:	
Personality:	

With your partner, act out one of these scenes with your two characters:

- waiting for a bus;
- on an aeroplane;
- in the supermarket;
- sitting on a bench in the park;
- in a fast-food restaurant.

Write the scene as a playscript.

Act it out with your partner using the script.

Does the dialogue reflect your character's personality?

Hint!

Write out your production notes like this:

Set: ....

Lighting: ....

Sound: ....

1   Look at the set design for the kitchen of Minna's house.

Write the production notes for this scene.

2 Read this outline of another scene in *Crummy Mummy and Me*.

Write production notes for this scene.

> Mum, Crusher, Minna and the baby are all sitting in the garden on a sunny day. They are all squashed into Minna's half of the garden, because Mum's half is too disgusting to sit in.
>
> A stray dog comes through the back hedge and Minna tries to get it out of the garden. A man then comes to buy Crusher's old car which is parked in the driveway next to the garden.
>
> At first, Crusher can't find his keys, but Minna eventually finds them where the dog has buried them under her flowers.
>
> Crusher shows the man how the car works, and accidentally runs over the dog. The man buys the car and the dog is buried in the back garden.

3 Read this passage from *Crummy Mummy and Me*.

Write production notes for this scene.

As soon as school was finished, I ran straight home. Even though it was a beautiful day, Mum was inside, sitting on a sofa with Crusher Maggot, watching the video and munching crisps. Crummy Dummy was jumping up and down in her cot as usual, trying to bump her head on the ceiling.

"What are you watching?"

"Horror film," Mum said. "*Curse of the Blood of Dracula.* Pass the fizzy."

I knew she meant the bottle on the table because that was redcurrant, and redcurrant was the colour that Crummy Dummy was dribbling.

From *Crummy Mummy and Me* by Anne Fine

1   Use these pictures to think of a plot for your play.

Use **copymaster 4** to plan your plot.

Think about:

Characters
Who are the main characters?
Will any other characters be involved?

Setting
Where does the action take place?

Problem
What has happened?
What is the new character telling Minna's family?
What happens next?
How is the problem resolved?

2 Use Minna's unfinished postcard to think of a plot for your play.

Dear Sara,

Having a fantastic time! We're sitting here on the beach, so I thought I'd drop you a line. The weather has been great and we've been swimming every day.

Yesterday we found some really strange footprints in the sand, and no-one could tell who or what they belonged to! Crusher said that he'd heard strange noises last night outside his tent, but I told him not to be such a baby – after all, there's nothing to be scared of here, is there?

Sara Green,
6 Copse Road,
Thornley,
Liverpool.

Use **copymaster 4** to plan your plot.

Think about:

Characters
Who are the main characters?
Will any other characters be involved?

Setting
Where does the action take place?

Problem
Why hasn't the postcard been finished?
What made the strange noises outside the tent?
What will happen next?

Write character profiles for the main characters in your play.
Draw pictures of your characters above the profiles.
Set them out in your book like this:

Name:

Age:

Appearance:

Personality:

Now use **copymaster 5** to plan each scene in your play.

ADDITIONAL SESSIONS

Writing in the style of Anne Fine

1 Copy this plan into your book.

Plan the middle and the end sections.

Think of a chapter title!

Chapter title _____

Beginning
Characters: Mum and Minna
Setting: inside the house
Problem: Minna is ill

Middle
1st event:
2nd event:
3rd event – conflict/climax:

End
Resolution:

2 Read the beginning of this chapter of *Crummy Mummy and Me*.

I've never been in trouble at school before. And, mind you, even this time it wasn't my fault. It was my mum's.

I may have mentioned to you before that, when it comes to getting me to school every day, and on time, my mum could do better. It's really up to me. If I didn't watch out for myself, I'd never get through the gates in the morning before the bell rings...

...Then, one day, I was really late. And that wasn't my fault, either. It was Mum's.

It happened on Tuesday...

From *Crummy Mummy and Me* by Anne Fine

What is the problem?
What do you think happens next?
Plan the rest of the chapter.
Give your chapter a title.

3   Look at the chapter headings and the picture.

Use one of them to plan a new chapter for *Crummy Mummy and Me*.

Think about the characters, setting and a problem.

What events do you think Anne Fine would have put in her chapter?

Our Pet

A Really Boring Ride in the Country

Keeping a reading journal

1 Use **copymaster 7** for your reading journal.

2 Make your own reading journal!
Answer these questions about a book you are reading.
You can also write down any other thoughts you might have!

Title ....
Author ....
Date Started ....
Date Finished ....
Cover/Blurb ....

Why did you choose this book?
How did the cover/blurb attract you?
Who are the main characters?
Write down any words which you find interesting or unusual.

After you have read the first chapter
Comment on your first feelings about the book.
Is the book how you expected it to be?
Who are the most interesting characters? How do you expect them to develop?
Is the plot interesting, and can you predict what is going to happen?

When you have read half of the book
Comment on your feelings half-way through the book.
Have any new characters been introduced? Why?
Has the pace of the book changed?
Has it become more or less exciting?
Can you predict how the book is going to end?

When you have finished the book
Comment on your feelings at the end of the book.
Were the characters how you expected them to be?
Did anything unusual happen in the story?
   Did you predict the main events?
Did you like the author's style? Why? Why not?
Would you read another book by the same
   author or in the same style? Why? Why not?

2 How to write

a recount for two different audiences

1 Looking at a historical recount

1 Use **copymaster 8**.

2 Read this recount. Then copy the table on page 21 into your book.

Fill it in with **key points** from the text.

ARCHIMEDES AND THE ROMANS

By 215 BC Rome had grown from a handful of villages to become the most powerful city in Italy, and was developing ambitions to build an empire. For a few years, however, the genius of the Greek philosopher Archimedes kept them at bay.

First of all, the Romans attacked the rich Greek city of Syracuse in Sicily, which lay to the south of Italy. In response, Archimedes invented a massive catapult, which shot huge stones at the Roman army and ships so they could not get near to the city walls. Archimedes's catapults kept the Romans out of Syracuse for three years.

Then, in 213 BC, Archimedes came up with another invention to halt the Roman advance. He set up large mirrors along the harbour walls, which reflected the sun on to nearby Roman ships and set them on fire.

By 211 BC, however, the Romans finally broke through the Greek defences and brought terror to the citizens of Syracuse. Archimedes was killed by a Roman soldier.

It was the beginning of the end for the Greeks. In the space of thirty years, all Greek cities had been conquered by the unstoppable Roman war machine.

Who?	What?	Where?	When?	Why?	How?

3 Now look at these extra sentences.

Which section of the recount does each sentence belong to – **orientation**, **events** or **reorientation**? Write the answers in your book.

The first one has been done for you.

1 By the 190s, half of the known world had been conquered by the Romans. = *reorientation*

2 The Roman soldier who killed Archimedes was punished for disobeying his commander's orders.

3 Archimedes's stand against the Romans lasted four years.

4 Archimedes also designed huge cranes which dropped heavy stones on the Roman ships.

5 Archimedes was a brainy guy who invented the coolest weapons to beat the Romans.

6 After a siege of eight months, the Romans marched into Syracuse where they easily defeated its starving and helpless inhabitants.

Can you find any sentences which are not suitable for a 'textbook' recount?

4 Read this recount. Then copy the table on page 23 into your book.

Fill it in with **key points** from the text.

The Battle of Salamis

For more than twenty years, Persia had attempted to conquer Greece and, in the summer of 480 BC, it seemed likely to succeed.

The Persian Emperor Xerxes, armed with 200,000 soldiers and 1,000 warships, forced his way past stubborn Spartan defenders at Thermopylai to occupy first Africa and then Athens itself.

The citizens of Athens managed to escape just before the Persian invaders arrived. Fortunately one of their leaders, Thermistocles, had persuaded the Athenian government to build a brand new fleet of triremes, which helped the citizens escape to nearby coasts.

Next, Thermistocles ordered the Greek triremes to sail into a narrow stretch of water in the bay of Salamis. This clever plan worked, as the Persians thought the Greeks were retreating, and followed them into the bay. Trapped in the narrow bay, the Persian ships had no room to manoeuvre, and were smashed to pieces by the rams on the front of the Greek triremes. Xerxes and his men retreated back to Asia.

The following year, in 479 BC, the Greeks again defeated Xerxes at the Battle of Plotea. Xerxes's ambitions of conquering the Greeks were in ruins.

For the next fifty years, with the Persian threat removed, Greek culture flourished as it never has before or since.

Who?	What?	Where?	When?	Why?	How?

5 Now look at these extra sentences.

Which section of the recount does each sentence belong to – **orientation**, **events** or **reorientation**? Write the answers in your book.

The first one has been done for you.

1 First of all, Thermistocles went to the temple at Delphi to ask advice from the 'Oracle' – an adviser on behalf of the gods. = *events*

2 The wars between Greece and Persia began when Darius I, the Persian King, expanded his vast empire to include Greek colonies on the coast of what is now Turkey.

3 Xerxes watched the sea battle from a throne on the shore.

4 So then Xerxes arrives in Athens, sees that it's deserted and decides to burn down all the buildings.

5 Fifty years later, a bloody civil war began between the Athenians and Spartans.

6 Not for the first or last time, the Greeks used their cunning to defeat the enemy.

Can you find any sentences which are not suitable for a 'textbook' recount?

1 Look at these two extracts.
Identify which is from a **letter** and which is from a **newspaper**.
In your book, write down two reasons for each choice.

> ### *TEACHER DIES AFTER HEMLOCK OVERDOSE*
>
> *The teacher and philosopher Socrates died yesterday after drinking poison made from the hemlock plant.*
>
> *A judge said when he heard the news, "He will not be missed. His teaching was corrupting the young."*

Socrates drank the poison quickly and cheerfully. Until then most of us had held back our tears. But when we saw him drinking, the tears came in floods. I covered my face and wept – not for him but for myself. I had lost such a good friend.

2 Rewrite this passage as *either* a newspaper article *or* a letter to someone you know.

The race called the 'marathon' gets its name from the Battle of Marathon between the Greeks and the Persians. After the battle, a soldier called Pheidippides ran back from Marathon to Athens, to bring news of the Greek victory. He ran the 26 miles to Athens, delivered his message and then dropped down dead.

3 Look at the extracts about different historical periods on this page and on page 26.

Identify which is from a **letter**, a **newspaper** and a **textbook**.

In your book, write down two reasons for each choice.

That same night after dinner my Lord of Hunsdon drew me to a quiet gallery that I might hear some music, where I might hear the Queen play upon the virginals. After I had hearkened a while, I took by the tapestry that hung before the door of the chamber, and seeing that her back was toward the door, I

entered within the chamber and stood still and heard her play excellently well. But she left off as she turned her about and saw me.

From *Tudors (History Insights)* by Donna Bailey

The Wessex Saxons washed their swords in Viking blood last night to celebrate a vital victory. And the surprise star of the battle was ex-king Athelwulf's youngest son, Alfred. The Danes were a favourite in the fight and held the high ground. But Alfred went at them 'like a wild boar', one witness raved. The bloody battle raged around a single stunted thorn bush. Saxons and Danes swapped places as both tried to hit that hilly height. At last the sword-swinging Saxons drove the desperate Danes back to their camp until darkness stopped the slaughter.

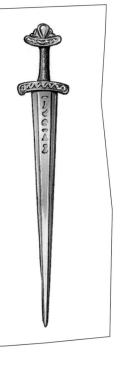

From *The Vicious Vikings* by Terry Deary

A few of the Victorian poor rose to great heights, but it helped to go abroad, where there were more opportunities and less prejudice against people from poor backgrounds.

Andrew Carnegie left Scotland in 1848 as a boy of thirteen with his parents, and sailed to America in an old whaling ship of 800 tons, the *Wiscasset*.

When he arrived in America he started out as a messenger boy, then a salesman, then a broker, then a railwayman. Finally he became owner of a huge iron and steel company that dominated United States industry, making full use of the cheap labour of all his fellow immigrants.

In 1901, the same year that Queen Victoria died, he sold out and spent the next eighteen years giving away 350 million dollars of his own money. It was a great American success story.

From *Queen Victoria* by Fred Finney

4 Choose one of the extracts on this page or on page 25. Rewrite it in a different recount style (letter, newspaper or textbook).

Planning a newspaper recount

1   Use **copymaster 9** to plan your historical newspaper recount.

2   Plan your historical newspaper recount.
Remember to plan notes for:

- an orientation section
- the main events
- a reorientation section
- an illustration
- a caption to go with the illustration

Another great victory for Alexander

King Henry to marry <u>again</u>

1   Use **copymaster 10** to plan your historical letter recount.

2   Plan your historical letter recount.
Remember to include:

- greeting and closure
- an orientation section
- the main events
- a reorientation section
- personal comments and opinions

ADDITIONAL SESSIONS

Note-making and abbreviations

1 Match these words to their common abbreviations.

and	=
a quarter	i.e.
plus	∴
equals	e.g.
therefore	+
for example	2nd
second	&
that is	$\frac{1}{4}$

2 Write these sentences in note form. Use abbreviations wherever you can.

1 The first Olympic Games were held in 776 BC.

2 They were held every four years and continued for a thousand years.

3 The Games were held in a sacred valley called Olympia.

4 There were lots of events, for example running, wrestling and discus throwing.

5 The ancient Olympic Games finally stopped because the Romans did not want them.

6 The modern Olympic Games began in 1896.

3 Write these sentences in note form. Use abbreviations wherever you can.

1 The first Greek plays were performed around about the sixth century BC.

2 There were many famous Greek playwrights, for example Sophocles and Euripedes.

3 The Greeks were lucky that their weather was good because all plays were performed outside.

4 The biggest theatre in Athens could seat fifteen thousand people, and might have as many as five plays a day!

5 The Greeks wrote tragic and comic plays, as well as *satyrs,* comedies where the chorus dressed as satyrs with goat legs and ears.

6 Sophocles's play *Oedipus Tyrannus* is a very famous Greek tragedy.

7 There were no women in Greek plays – male actors also played the female parts.

8 Actors would wear face masks and high platform shoes, so they moved around very slowly.

Writing and testing instructions

Write instructions to make or do something.
Here are some ideas:

- making a paper aeroplane;
- playing hopscotch;
- using a computer to make a birthday card;
- making a mobile for the classroom.

Now swap your instructions with another group.
Follow the new instructions. How well do they work?

Hint!

When testing instructions, think about the following:

- Is there a 'What you need' section?
- Are the instructions in the right order?
- Are all the steps included?
- Do the instructions start with a verb?
- How could you improve the instructions?

How to write
a legend

1 Beginnings and settings

1 Read the beginning of this story from Siberia.

Long, long ago, there was a terrible storm. First, a strong wind began to blow. Then thunder boomed and lightning flashed across the sky. Last of all, the freezing rain pelted down, on and on and on.

Everyone was soaked through and icy cold. Oh, imagine how miserable they were! Imagine how the children cried!

"Please, please," they shouted to the dark sky, "someone make the storm stop!"

In the village there was a man called Big Raven who could work magic. Big Raven heard the children crying. He watched the storm for a long time, thinking, thinking hard.

From The Weather Drum by Rosalind Kerven

In your book, write answers to these questions:

- **When** did this take place?
- **Where** did it happen?
- **Who** are the characters?
- **Why** are they there?

2 Write about how the setting makes you feel.
Write down words or phrases that you think are powerful.

3 Here are two passages which describe settings.
Write about how each one makes you feel.
Write down words or phrases that you think are powerful.

THESEUS AND THE MINOTAUR

Through the cunning labyrinth he stole, this way and that, listening intently for any sound the hidden monster might make. Suddenly he heard the sound of snorting and the scuffling of some clumsy body. He judged that the Minotaur must be round the next corner of the passage he was exploring.

From *Heroes and Monsters* by James Reeves

Beowulf and the Dragon

A windswept moor reached up to the headland of Eagleness. That was a desolate place, a prow of land jutting out into the ocean, precipitous, riddled with caves. All the land round about had been laid waste; it looked like fields of stubble fired after harvesting.

From *Beowulf* by Kevin Crossley-Holland

4 Choose one passage. Think about how it begins.
Use other sources of information to answer these questions.

- **When** did this take place?
- **Where** did it happen?
- **Who** are the characters?
- **Why** are they there?

Draw a table like this in your book:

Size	Strange features	Sounds	Actions	Powers

1 Read the next part of the story about Big Raven.
Pick out words which describe him and put them in the correct section of your table.

At last, he went to fetch his special coat. This coat was made of feathers, and its arms were shaped like wings. He put it on and turned himself into a huge, black bird! Then Big Raven flew straight up to the Sky.

From *The Weather Drum* by Rosalind Kerven

2 Use the information in your table to draw and label a picture of Big Raven.

3 Choose two descriptions of characters on page 35.

For each one, fill in your table with words from the text.

4 Read all the descriptions of characters on page 35.

For each one, fill in your table with words from the text.

From *Heroes and Monsters* by James Reeves

THESEUS AND THE MINOTAUR

He saw the great black head, the cruel horns, the wicked eyes, and even Theseus's heart began to thump. Nevertheless, he tightened his grip on the sword and awaited the charge that must surely come. Sure enough, the Minotaur lowered its head, gave a terrifying bellow and rushed towards Theseus.

Beowulf and the Dragon

At once a gust of smoke issued from the cave; the cave itself snarled. As the dragon slithered down the slope towards him, Beowulf brandished his sword, Naegling. He slashed at the serpent's neck, but he could not pierce its scale-corslet. Flames leapt through the air, brighter than day's bright light; Beowulf sheltered behind his shield.

...They marvelled at the loathsome dragon, its scales burnished orange and brown and green, its coils and folded wings, its forked tongue. One man measured it, fifty paces from head to tail.

From *Beowulf* by Kevin Crossley-Holland

PERSEUS AND MEDUSA

She had the form of a once beautiful girl, but her brazen claws and sharp teeth proclaimed her a monster. Beneath the frowning brows her fierce eyes  were closed in sleep, but amidst her tangled locks a hundred serpents hissed and writhed. No wonder men had been turned to stone at the mere sight of so terrible a creature.

From *Heroes and Monsters* by James Reeves

5   Choose one of the characters in your table.
Draw a labelled picture of it.

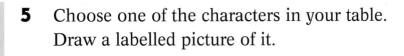

powder

scissors

polished shield

sack

string

angry dog

drum

invisibilty cloak

winged sandals

harp

Draw a table like this in your book:

Problem	Resolution

1 Using your table, write down the **problem** in the Big Raven legend. Now write what you think the **resolution** might be.

(**Clue!** Big Raven uses one of the objects on this page.)

2 Using your table, write down the **problem** in the Theseus legend. Now write what you think the **resolution** might be.

(**Clue!** Theseus uses two of the objects on this page.)

3 Using your table, write down the **problem** in the Perseus legend. Now write what you think the **resolution** might be.

(**Clue!** Perseus uses three of the objects on this page.)

4   Use **copymaster 12**.

5   Look at these pictures from *Odysseus and the Cyclops*.
Write sentences to describe what happens in each picture.

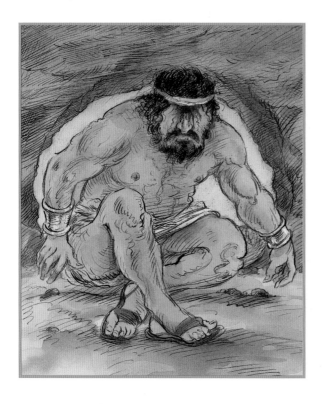

1 Use **copymaster 13** to plan an extraordinary character and setting for your legend.

2 Now draw a picture of your character in his or her setting. Use your plan on **copymaster 13** to label the picture.

Here is a picture to help you. It shows the Cyclops on his island.

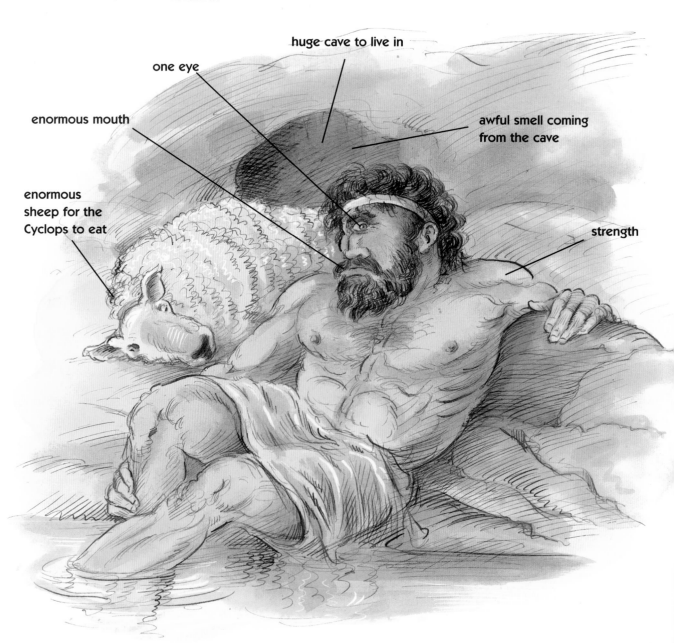

huge cave to live in

one eye

enormous mouth

awful smell coming from the cave

enormous sheep for the Cyclops to eat

strength

5 Planning the legend

1 Use **copymaster 14** to plan your legend.

2 Draw a framework like this in your book. Use it to plan your legend.

Beginning
Hero/heroine

Extraordinary character

Setting

Problem

Middle
Events

Climax

Ending
Resolution

Conclusion

Writing a poem to accompany the legend

1 Copy this framework into your book.

Complete it to make a poem for your own extraordinary character.

Then think of a title!

Hear me, _____ ,

_____,

_____

great god of the _____!

Send me _____, send me _____,

send me _____, _____;

send me _____ too _____

for the skies to contain!

May _____

_____ with your _____,

close round Odysseus

and his fine men;

may they _____

may they _____;

may they never set foot

on their own lands

                again!

Based on 'The Cyclops' Revenge' by Judith Nicholls

2 Make up a completely new revenge poem for your own extraordinary character to say.

Matching writing to the needs of the reader

Imagine you are Odysseus! Write a postcard to Penelope, describing where you have landed.

Use **copymaster 15**. Draw your setting on the other side.

Use this checklist to help you:

- Use an appropriate greeting and closure.
- Think about what information Penelope would want to hear.
- Include personal details.
- Put the address on the right-hand side. Write it in the correct order.

4 How to write

a non-chronological report with explanation

1 Analysing key features

1 You need **copymaster 16**.

Look at 'The Solar System' text on OHT/posters 18 and 19. Copy the heading on to the framework on the copymaster.

Now read these six sentences.

Decide where each sentence fits best into the report. Write each one on the copymaster under the correct heading.

1 The word 'planet' comes from a Greek word meaning 'wanderer'.

2 The temperature on the surface of the Sun is about 5,500°C (9,900°F).

3 In one second, the Sun gives off 13 million times more energy than all the electricity used in the USA in one year.

4 The first artificial satellite, *Sputnik 1*, was launched into orbit around the Earth in 1957.

5 Meteors are stones or rocks that that have fallen away from asteroids and comets.

6 Mars has two moons.

2 You need **copymaster 17**.

Organise the information into sections to fit the three-part framework:

- opening section;
- main section (think of some sub-headings);
- closing section.

3 You need **copymasters 17 and 18**.

Organise all the information into sections to fit the three-part framework.

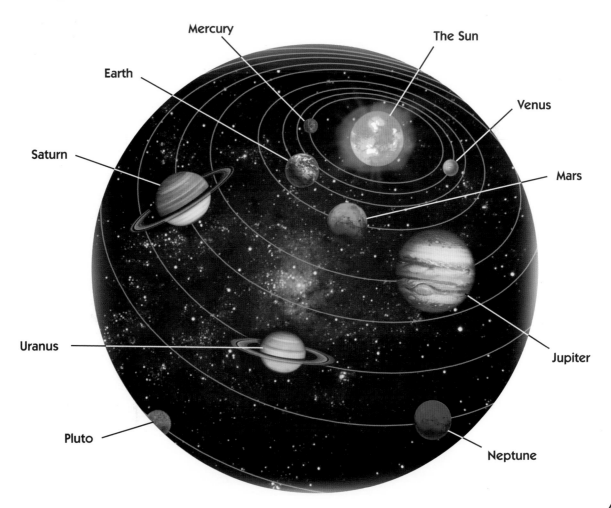

1 Match these words from 'The Solar System' report with their glossary definitions.

asteroid	the force of attraction that exists between two large bodies
orbit	the path of a body through space, often around another strongly attracting body
axis	gives off energy that travels in the form of waves or particles
gravitational pull	a minor planet
radiates	a real or imaginary line through the centre of a spinning object

Now write your own glossary definition for these two words. Use a dictionary.

comet
satellite

2 Make this text sound better by using **pronouns** and **connectives** where appropriate.

Write the new text in your book.

The Moon is Earth's satellite. The Moon is 4.6 billion years old. The Moon is the same age as Earth.

The Moon has no atmosphere. The Moon has no water.

The temperatures on the sunny side of the Moon are near boiling. The temperatures on the dark side of the Moon are lower than any on Earth.

The main features of the Moon were first seen in 1609 by Galileo. The main features of the Moon are dark plains, mountain ranges and ring-like craters. The Moon's craters were formed by meteors that crashed into its surface.

The first man to walk on the Moon was Neil Armstrong. Neil Armstrong first walked on the Moon on 20th July 1969.

---

3 Look at the information you put in the right order in the last session. Write out this information on **copymaster 16**.

Try to link the sentences together using **pronouns** and **connectives**.

4 The author of this report got very confused. The paragraphs are all mixed up.

Write down the letters of the sections in the correct order.

Then think of a suitable title and sub-headings for your finished report.

a Wood is a tough natural material produced by trees. Wood is strong but light. Wood is classified as hard or soft, depending on the type of tree it comes from. Wood is often burned as a fuel.

b Modern life depends on the use of many different materials. People use materials to build homes, make clothes, cook food and to do a wide range of complicated jobs. Different types of material have different qualities – called **properties** – that make them suitable for different uses.

c Metals are natural materials. Most metals are strong and hard and can resist damage in everyday use. Metals can be bent and shaped for various purposes. Most metals make good electrical conductors.

d Natural and synthetic materials need to be used carefully. Wood should be replaced by planting more trees. Many metals and plastics can be recycled.

e Plastics are artificial materials manufactured from a variety of natural and synthetic resins. Plastics are very strong and light. Plastics are waterproof and do not rust. Plastics can be moulded or extruded into many different shapes. Plastics are good electrical insulators.

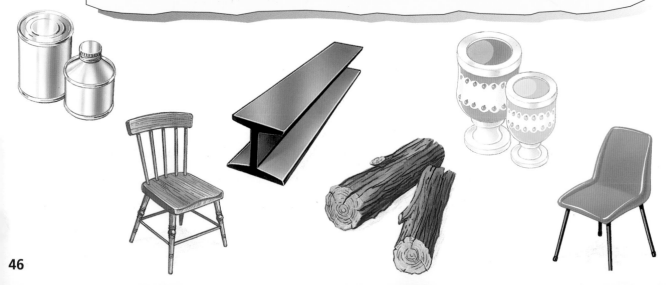

Hint!

How to write a good report

Don't...
- give personal opinions;
- use adjectives that show your opinion (e.g. lovely, bad, interesting);
- use the kind of language that you would use with a friend.

Do...
- stick to facts;
- try to use the correct vocabulary for the subject;
- use formal language.

Sally knows a lot about science but she is very bad at writing reports! Michael knows nothing about science but he is good at writing formal language.

1 Some of these sentences were written by Sally and some by Michael. Write *S* for Sally's sentences and *M* for Michael's, for example *1 = S*.

Then rewrite Sally's sentences so that they are more appropriate for a report.

1 Mars is the nearest neighbour of Earth.
2 It has got really, really high rugged mountains.
3 I suppose it is called the 'red planet' because it has got red sand.
4 There are deep craters caused by asteroid strikes.
5 It is a mega-big planet – loads bigger than Earth.
6 Mars is often hidden by storm clouds of yellow dust.
7 I think Mars has two moons called Phobos and Deimos.

2 Oh dear! Sally has gone ahead and written a report about the planet Jupiter without waiting for Michael to help!

Can you put things right? This paragraph needs editing to make it formal and impersonal.

Discuss with a partner the changes you need to make. Then write the improved report in your book.

Jupiter is the greatest! Wow! It's the largest planet in the whole solar system. It is not a solid planet. It is a gas giant consisting mainly of helium and hydrogen. You couldn't stand on its surface, because it isn't solid, so you'd just sink right in. What a horrible thought! Jupiter's weather is pretty stormy. The atmosphere contains water, ammonia and methane. The surface of the planet is hidden beneath weird swirling gas clouds. The clouds are pretty pastel colours. Amongst the clouds is the famous Great Red Spot, a funny shaped swirly patch of ochre-coloured stuff. The planet has got these nearly invisible rings of circulating dust and debris whizzing round it. It also has at least sixteen larger satellites, including four named moons. It is weird to think that life could develop on Jupiter in the distant future, like scientists say it could.

3 Sally has given Michael a list of facts about Saturn. She has persuaded him to write the report for her! What do you think Michael would write?

Discuss with a partner which order to put the facts in. What kind of language will you need to write up the report?

Finally, write the report in your book.

Saturn
- cold gas giant
- planet composed mainly of hydrogen, helium, methane and ammonia
- clearly visible planetary rings – most famous feature
- over 100,000 separate rings around the equator
- rings are 5 metres deep, travelling rapidly
- Titan – one of main moons – large enough to have own atmosphere
- second largest planet
- rings are made of debris, particles of dust, frozen gases and crystals of water ice
- rings look like wide multi-coloured bands
- rings can be seen by telescope
- planet has many moons

ADDITIONAL SESSION

Writing up personal notes for others to read

1 Write these sentences in note form.

> **1** Mercury is really a very small planet. It is approximately one eighteenth of the size of the Sun.
>
> **2** Mercury and Venus are a great deal nearer to the Sun than our planet Earth is.
>
> **3** Venus is a very bright planet, and is in fact the brightest object in the sky except for the Sun and Moon.
>
> **4** Pluto is by far the most distant planet from the Sun and is very cold indeed.
>
> **5** Pluto's moon, which is called Charon, is approximately one half the size of the planet.

Compare your notes with a partner. What differences are there?

2 Write out one of the texts on page 51 in note form. Try to think of common ways of shortening some of the words, or familiar symbols you could use to replace them.

When you have finished, swap notes with someone who worked on the other text. See if you can understand each other's notes.

The European Southern Observatory, La Silla, Chile

SATURN

Saturn is the second largest planet in the solar system. It is a gas giant, composed mainly of hydrogen, helium, methane and ammonia. Its most famous feature is its system of planetary rings. There are over one hundred thousand separate rings circling Saturn's equator. They are approximately five metres deep and made of rapidly travelling pieces of debris such as particles of dust, frozen gases and crystals of water ice. They appear as wide, multi-coloured bands, clearly visible through a telescope. Saturn also has many satellite moons. One of these, Titan, is large enough to have its own dense atmosphere.

VENUS

Venus is similar in size to Earth. However, it spins two hundred and forty times more slowly than Earth, has a much hotter temperature at around four hundred and seventy degrees Celsius, and it has no moon. It is surrounded by yellow clouds. The yellow colour is caused by sulphuric acid, therefore scientists believe it may have volcanoes which are still active. Venus orbits the Sun in a clockwise direction, unlike the other planets in Earth's solar system which orbit in an anti-clockwise direction. It has been suggested by some astronomers that this may be because it was knocked upside down by another planet or an asteroid.

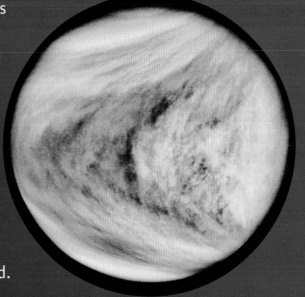

3 Look at the notes you have just made. Make them even shorter, as if they were personal notes that only you need to understand.

5 How to write

a performance poem

1 Analysing key features

1 Copy this table into your book. Fill in examples from 'The Adventures of Isabel'.

Key features of performance poetry	Tick if you find an example in the poem.	Copy some examples from the poem.
Rhythm: a strong beat, easy to clap out		
Rhyme: simple repetitive scheme		
Repetition: repeated words and phrases		
Use of direct speech, dialogue		
Direct address to the audience		

Boo!

2 You need **copymaster 20**.

Fill in the table with examples from the poems on pages 53 and 54.

You will soon be writing your own performance poem. Which features do you think will be the hardest to use in your text?

Jim

Jim was taken on a visit to the zoo, but was naughty and ran away...

He hadn't gone a yard when – Bang!
With open jaws a lion sprang,
And hungrily began to eat
The boy: beginning at his feet.

Now, just imagine how it feels
When first your toes and then your heels,
And then by gradual degrees,
Your shins and ankles, calves and knees,
Are slowly eaten, bit by bit.
No wonder Jim detested it!
No wonder that he shouted "Hi!"
The honest keeper heard his cry,
Though very fat he almost ran
To help the little gentleman.
"Ponto!" he ordered as he came
(for Ponto was the lion's name),
"Ponto" he cried, with angry frown.
"Let go, Sir! Down, Sir! Put it down!"

From 'Jim' by Hilaire Belloc

The Charge of the Light Brigade

*The Light Brigade was a cavalry regiment that
was ordered into a narrow valley to charge the
enemy guns...*

Half a league, half a league,
Half a league onward,
All in the valley of Death
Rode the six hundred.
"Forward, the Light Brigade!
Charge for the guns!" he said:
Into the valley of Death
Rode the six hundred.

Cannon to right of them,
Cannon to left of them,
Cannon in front of them
Volley'd and thunder'd;
Storm'd at with shot and shell,
Boldly they rode and well,
Into the jaws of Death,
Into the mouth of Hell
Rode the six hundred.

From 'The Charge of the Light Brigade' by Lord Tennyson

3 You need **copymaster 20**.

Fill in the table with examples from the poems on this page and on page 56.

Can you guess which of these poems is by Ogden Nash?

Give reasons for your choice.

The Song of Hiawatha

Then Iagoo, the great boaster,
He the marvellous story-teller,
He the traveller and the talker,
He the friend of old Nokomis,
Made a bow for Hiawatha;
From a branch of ash he made it,
From an oak-bough made the arrows,
Tipped with flint, and winged with feathers,
And the cord he made of deer-skin.
Then he said to Hiawatha:
"Go, my son, into the forest,
Where the red-deer herd together,
Kill for us a famous roebuck,
Kill for us a deer with antlers!"

The Camel

The camel has a single hump;
The dromedary, two;
Or else the other way around.
I'm never sure. Are you?

Horatius

*The city of Rome was about to be
attacked by the Etruscan army...*

XX
Just then a scout came flying,
All wild with haste and fear:
"To arms! To arms! Sir Consul;
Lars Porsena is here."
On the low hills to westward,
The Consul fixed his eye,
And saw the swarthy storm of dust
Rise fast along the sky.

XXI
And nearer fast and nearer
Doth the red whirlwind come;
And louder still and still more loud,
From underneath that rolling cloud,
Is heard the trumpet's war-note proud,
The trampling, and the hum.
And plainly and more plainly
Now through the gloom appears,
Far to left and far to right,
In broken gleams of dark-blue light,
The long array of helmets bright
The long array of spears.

Analysing rhythm, rhyme and repetition

1   Look again at verses 1 and 3 of 'The Adventures of Isabel', on **copymaster 19**.

Tap out the rhythm and underline the stressed syllables.

Mark the rhyme scheme using different coloured pens.

Circle any examples of repetition you can find.

> Isabel met an enormous bear,
> Isabel, Isabel didn't care.

2   Look again at the two poems on **copymaster 21**.

Tap out the rhythm and underline the stressed syllables.

Mark the rhyme scheme using different coloured pens.

Circle any examples you can find of repetition and/or alliteration.

> He hadn't gone a yard when – Bang!
> With open jaws a lion sprang

3   Look again at the three poems on **copymaster 22**.

Tap out the rhythm and underline the stressed syllables.

Analyse the rhyme scheme of each poem using different coloured pens.

Circle any examples you can find of repetition and/or alliteration.

> Just then a scout came flying,
> All wild with haste and fear

1 Look at these pictures of four 'scary' characters.
Do you recognise them from stories and films?
Choose one or two to describe.

1

2

3

4

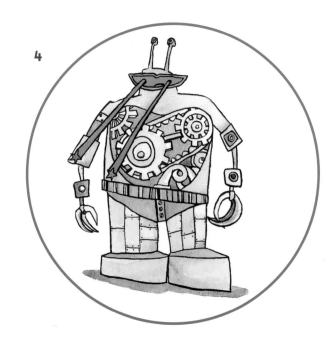

First think of words to describe the appearance, personality and actions of your characters. Choose unusual words.

Then find words to rhyme with the words in your list. Use your thesaurus (or a rhyming dictionary) to help you find interesting rhymes.

Write as many rhyming couplets as you can about your characters.

What adventures might Isabel have with each character? Look at this dragon example to give you some ideas.

Describing words	Rhyming words
• lives in a **cave**	brave save shave rave wave behave
• **scary**	hairy fairy wary vary
• **green** scaly skin	mean bean clean keen lean seen
• **red** eyes	bed dead said fed head
• long **claws**	paws pause bores jaws roars outlaws

Rhyming couplets

A   Isabel met a dragon in a cave
Isabel looked at him, bold and brave

or   Isabel met a dragon in a cave
Isabel didn't rant and rave

or   Isabel met a dragon in a cave
Isabel told him he'd better behave

B   The dragon was green, the dragon was scary
The dragon's feet were huge and hairy

or   The dragon was scary, the dragon was green
The scariest dragon that she'd ever seen

2 Have a go at writing like Ogden Nash. Use this verse framework to help you write a new verse about Isabel.

First introduce a scary character or a 'bugaboo'. Say something about what it looks like or where Isabel met it. Describe how she reacted. Remember to make the lines rhyme:

> Isabel met _____,
> Isabel _____.

Now write another rhyming couplet to describe the scary character:

> The _____ was _____, the _____ was _____,
> _____.

Now write what it said to Isabel:

> The _____ said, _____,
> _____.

Here comes the chorus:

> Isabel, Isabel didn't worry,
> Isabel didn't scream or scurry,

Now, how did Isabel solve the problem? Remember to make it rhyme:

> She _____,
> Then Isabel _____.

See how many new verses you can come up with. Have fun!

3 One of Isabel's opponents was a doctor – a person who sometimes has to be 'cruel to be kind'.

Think of four more real-life characters, and the things they do that children don't always like. Make a list of them in your book. Choose one or two to develop further.

Think of some words to describe their appearance, behaviour and personality. Then find words to rhyme with the words in your list. Use a thesaurus and a rhyming dictionary to help you make these rhyming pairs as funny as possible.

Try using your pairs of words to write some entertaining couplets about your chosen characters. If you have time you could illustrate them.

Here are some examples:

> The dentist was nasty, the dentist was mean,
> He came at Kirsty with a drilling machine.

> The swimming coach had one silly rule,
> She wouldn't let children splash in the pool.

ADDITIONAL SESSION

Writing from another character's point of view

1 Imagine that you are Isabel's doctor. You are writing a letter to your colleague, Dr Curall. Use the writing frame below to help you.

What do you think your name might be? (Sign it at the bottom of the letter.)

[Address]

[Date]

Dear ____________________

I am writing to inform you of an ________________

event that occurred today at [place] ________________.

I arrived in order to ________________________________

____.

First ____

____________________. Then I ___________________________.

Suddenly something quite unexpected happened: ____

____.

I said: ____.

What happened next was that ________________________.

Finally, I ____.

The day's events made me feel _______________________.

Now I intend to _______________________________________.

Yours sincerely,

____

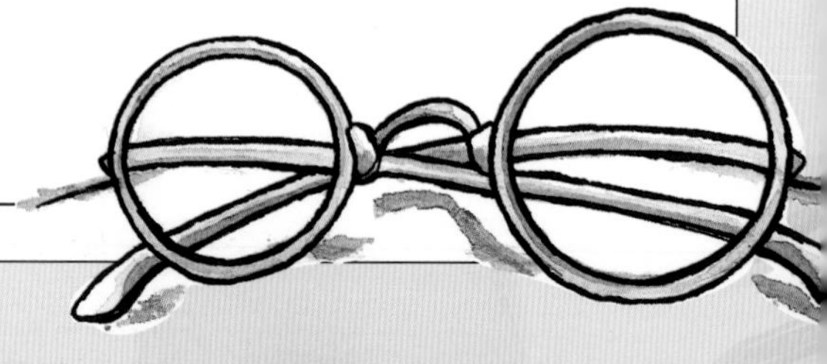

2 Re-read 'Jim' on page 53. What do you think happens next?

Find out by reading the next verse:

The lion made a sudden stop,
He let the dainty morsel drop,
And slunk reluctant to his cage,
Snarling with disappointed rage.
But when he bent him over Jim,
The honest keeper's eyes were dim.
The lion having reached his head,
The miserable boy was dead!

Now imagine that you are the lion keeper. Write a letter to your boss, the Zoo Manager.

Use the letter framework on page 62 to help you describe everything that happened, including Jim's death.

Invent names for yourself and for the Zoo Manager and use these in your letter.

3 Read 'Jim' on page 53. What do you think happened next? Find out by reading the next verse (above).

Now think about the incident from Ponto's point of view. (Ponto is the lion!)

You can use the letter framework on page 62 to help you, but imagine how Ponto would describe this incident orally to another inhabitant of the zoo.

Make notes about what you would say. Remember to include lots of personal thoughts and interpretations.

Rehearse your script, perhaps using a special voice for the lion.

Be ready to perform for the class!

6 How to write
a persuasive letter

1 How to use persuasive devices

1 Josintha is writing an article about exotic pets for her school magazine.

She has made a list of points to include.

> 1 I think it is cruel to take animals from their own habitat.
>
> 2 51% of captured exotic animals die before they become pets.
>
> 3 I don't think that pet shops take good care of exotic animals.
>
> 4 I know lots of vets who won't look after exotic animals.
>
> 5 The RSPCA has found exotic animals abandoned on the streets.
>
> 6 Exotic animals have food and water when they are being transported.
>
> 7 I think that exotic animals do not have enough food and water when they are being transported.
>
> 8 Environmental Health Officers inspect pet shops every year.

The editor tells her that she is only allowed to put facts in her article, not opinions. Can you help her to sort them out?

Write two headings: 'Facts' and 'Opinions'. Then write the number for each sentence under the right heading.

Hint!

Facts are not written using 'I'.

2 Look at these pictures of exotic animals.

Write two captions for each picture, one as an exotic pet owner and one as someone who is against keeping animals as pets.

The first one has been done for you.

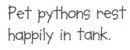

Pet pythons rest happily in tank.

Starving pythons kept in terrible conditions.

3 This article appeared in the *Cardiff Daily Post*.

Decide whether you are *for* or *against* keeping exotic pets.

Rewrite the headline and the article so that it supports your point of view.

Think about:

- which facts you want to use;
- writing opinion as fact;
- changing facts to include opinion;
- using half-truths.

Hint!

Here are some useful persuasive devices:

Bias: select only the facts that support your point of view.

State opinions as facts: remember not to write these using 'I...'!

Manipulate facts: use words that reflect your opinion (e.g. '*cruelly* captured') and use **half-truth** (e.g. 51% = most!).

SHOULD WE KEEP EXOTIC PETS?

For many years people only kept cats, dogs or goldfish as pets but now lots of pet owners have more exotic animals in their homes. Snakes, lizards, spiders and turtles are just some of the animals which are now being kept as pets.

These animals are often captured in their own habitat and transported to this country in crates. Food and water is provided for their journey. However, 51% of the animals die before they become pets.

Pet shop owners do not legally require any qualifications to look after exotic animals. Environmental Health Officers inspect pet shops every year. The RSPCA has found animals in poor conditions in pet shops and in 1998–1999, 68 pet shop owners and staff were convicted of cruelty.

There are no statistics to show how many animals are well cared for as pets. The RSPCA have found exotic animals abandoned on the street by owners who could no longer look after them.

Should we keep exotic pets? Write and tell us what *you* think.

1 Use copymaster 24.
George is trying to persuade
his mum to let him have a
pet snake...

2 It was announced last week that a footballer in the Premier
League is being paid £50,000 per week. A local radio station
has been reporting on the story and interviewed Liverpool's
manager to find out his point of view.

Find the persuasive words and the linking words in his
argument. Write them in your book.

"I believe that
footballers should be paid a decent wage.
Some people think that footballers do not work hard
enough to earn their wages. However, the real truth is
that footballers train extremely hard, not only during the
season but also in their holiday times. What is more, they are
often required to play three or four matches per week.
Another reason that they are highly paid is that they are making
money for the club. People pay to see skilled players and buy shirts
with their names on. This brings in lots of money for the club to
spend on improving the ground and buying new players.
Surely everyone must agree that the players should
get a share of it?
Poor wages mean poor quality players. As a result
of this, football matches would be less
entertaining. Is this what
you really want to see?"

3 Use **copymaster 25**. It is an interview with a football fan who believes that footballers are paid too much.

4 The radio station now wants to interview a football fan who believes that footballers are paid too much. What do you think the fan might say?

Spend a few minutes noting down some arguments. Then take turns to be the fan and interview each other.

Make your argument clear and use some of the persuasive and linking words from your list.

You could record your argument on cassette or write it down in your book.

1 Use **copymaster 26**.

 2 Use **copymaster 27**.

3 Mr Zindani owns an iguana. He disagrees with Mrs Cooper and he is writing to the newspaper to put forward his own point of view. Can you help him to write his letter?

He has written some arguments for the middle of his letter, but they need putting in order. (Write down the letters in the right order.)

He also needs to write a suitable greeting and closure, and a first and last paragraph. (Write these in your book.)

---

a Furthermore, most people are perfectly capable of looking after exotic animals. They completely understand their diet and provide them with good living conditions.

---

b What is more, pet shop owners have to apply for licences before they can sell exotic animals. These controls are sufficient to ensure that animals in pet shops are well cared for.

---

c Of course, there are a few cases of neglect and cruelty, but there are also thousands of exotic pets who are well cared for and live happily with their owners.

---

d Firstly, exotic animals are transported according to regulations and provided with enough space and adequate food and water. They are captured humanely and many endangered animals are then bred in captivity to ensure that the species survives. Surely this is conservation, not destruction?

---

e Secondly, environmental health officers who can check that the animals have suitable living conditions, inspect pet shops every year.

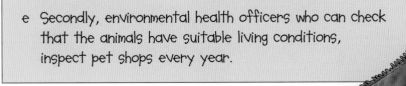

How to construct and present an argument

1 You are going on radio to speak against using performing animals in circuses.

Use this information to help you prepare your interview notes.

- Animals can be badly treated in circuses.
- Circus animals pace about and chew the bars of their cages. This shows that they are unhappy.
- Animals that are not needed are destroyed, sold or abandoned.
- The animals are kept in small, unsuitable pens.
- Some animals are taken from the wild to perform in circuses.
- People learn about animals by watching television, not by going to the circus.

Sort the information into sections:
- Capture
- Living conditions + care
- Education

Are there any further points you could add?

2   You are going to be interviewed on a radio programme about performing circus animals.

Read this information first.

- People learn a lot about animals by visiting circuses.
- Animals can be ill-treated or even die in circuses.
- Trained keepers and vets look after the circus animals.
- Circus animals can show abnormal behaviour such as pacing and chewing the bars of their cages.
- Animals that are not needed are destroyed, sold or abandoned.
- The animals are kept in spacious, clean enclosures.
- Some circus animals are taken from the wild.
- Some circuses give money to conservation centres for endangered animals.

Decide whether you are *for* or *against* using circus animals.

Choose the points that you will use in your argument. Write them in note form – for example:

For	Against
trained keepers and vets	animals ill-treated

Add any other information from your own research.

Next, decide which order you will present your points in and organise them under headings.

3   Now present your case to the rest of the group.
You could record your interview on cassette.

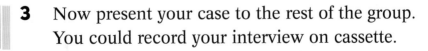

Hint!

Remember to organise your arguments into sections. Use these headings to help you.
  Purpose (*state my position*):
  Main points:
  Conclusion:

ADDITIONAL SESSIONS

How to make notes and organise information

1 You are going to support the view that performing animals should *not* be used in circuses.

Read this information from an animal welfare group.

Write down the points in note form under two headings – 'Training' and 'Living conditions'.

Remember just to write the **key words**.

- Animals taken from the wild are often beaten with whips and clubs.
- Big cats are kept in wagons for over 90% of the time.
- Between performances, animals are kept in small cages with just enough room for them to turn around and lie down.
- To teach bears to walk upright, their front paws may be burned.
- Elephants are tied by a front or hind leg for over 60% of the time.
- Outside, animals are tied to the ground or kept in small pens.
- Children screamed and families walked out when tigers were beaten during a performance by a well-known circus in Surrey.

Now write up your notes as full sentences.

2 Read extract 1 on page 73. Use the information to support the view that performing animals should *not* be used in circuses.

Make notes, and organise the notes into three sections – 'Capture', 'Training' and 'Living conditions'.

3 Read extracts 1 and 2 on page 73. They are taken from the websites of two animal welfare groups.
Use the information to support the view that performing animals should *not* be used in circuses.
Make notes and then organise them into sections, giving each section a title.

Extract 1

 Animal performances in circuses are becoming less popular. But many circuses still use animals, treating them as curiosities, like the dwarfs and bearded ladies of the side-shows not so long ago.

 Animals taken from the wild are often beaten into submission with whips and clubs to break their spirit and 'show them who is boss'. To teach bears to walk on their hind legs, their front paws may be burned.

 Between performances the animals are housed in cages which are small for ease of transport, leaving just enough room for the animals to turn around and lie down. Outside the cages, animals are tied to the ground or kept in small pens.

 Many animals in circuses are wild animals whose natural environment cannot be recreated in an artificial environment.

From: www.safe.org.nz

Extract 2

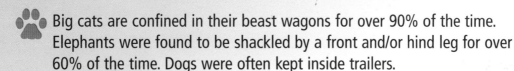 Big cats are confined in their beast wagons for over 90% of the time. Elephants were found to be shackled by a front and/or hind leg for over 60% of the time. Dogs were often kept inside trailers.

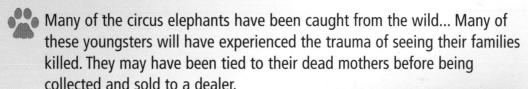 Many of the circus elephants have been caught from the wild... Many of these youngsters will have experienced the trauma of seeing their families killed. They may have been tied to their dead mothers before being collected and sold to a dealer.

 A well-known circus promoter was fined £1000 for transporting a lion cub in an overcrowded and unfit container. The cub was found to be paralysed.

 Children screamed and cried and families walked out when tigers were beaten with sticks during a performance by a well-known circus at a site in Surrey.

From: www.caps-uk.dircon.co.uk

How to write a persuasive leaflet

Ed has seen this leaflet posted up around Rossington

1 Imagine that you are Ed, preparing to open your exotic pet shop.

Use the following arguments to design a leaflet to convince people that 'Ed's Exotic Pets' *should* be allowed to open.

Write a 'catchy' heading.

Think carefully about what pictures you want to use.

> ● Impress your friends by owning an exotic animal!
> ● All our animals are captured carefully.
> ● Animals are looked after by trained staff in the shop.
> ● Exotic animals are easy to keep.
> ● Vets will treat all animals.

2 Imagine that you are Ed, preparing to open your exotic pet shop.

Design a leaflet to convince people that 'Ed's Exotic Pets' *should* be allowed to open.

Think about:

- a 'catchy' heading;
- how to organise your argument in bullet points;
- the size of writing for each section;
- what kind of pictures you will use.

Before starting work, **stop** and **think**.

To help you get ready for writing, consider the following questions:

Who is your **audience**?

What is the **purpose** of your text?

What **text type** will it be? (Be careful!
You might need to combine two types.)

How will you **structure** the text?

How will you **sequence and link** the text?

What sort of **information** or **ideas** should the text contain?

What sort of **language** will you use?

What star ways can you think of to **impress the marker**?

Now make a quick **plan**.

Make **brief notes** about what information and ideas will go into each main section of the text. You should aim to include:

- an opening section
- the main section
- a concluding section

1 You have decided to re-read a favourite book. As you turn the pages, you are surprised to find a beautiful colour illustration that was not there before! You stare at it for a moment. Before your eyes, the colours swim and blur… and one of the characters steps out of the book and begins speaking to you! Write a short story about what happens next…

Your favourite book might be be an adventure, a mystery, a historical story or science fiction. You can base your story on a real book, or make up one of your own.

2 My Finest Hour!

Yes! I had finally done it. All the time spent in preparation had paid off. Everyone around me was cheering and I felt like a star. I knew today was going to be special when…

Can you continue this story about the moment of your dreams?

3 Imagine you are an alien spy sending information to your emperor on the planet Zxarg. Your mission has been to find out as much as possible about Earthlings. Write a report about this.

Remember to include all the important details about people on Earth – what they look like, how their bodies work, what kind of homes they live in… and as many other headings as you need.

Write in a formal, impersonal style to show respect for your emperor!

4 There are plans to build a large factory in your town. The chosen site is Hollybush Park, a popular green area that has recently been neglected and vandalised. Something needs to be done with the park, but should it be used for leisure or industry? All your friends and family have a different point of view.

Your job is to write a letter to your local councillor, Ms Angel Goodbody, who has promised to act on the wishes of the community. You must explain the range of views in the community, but make your own side of the argument seem much stronger. Tell her what *you* want to happen to the park.

Present a well-argued case in support of your opinion. Good luck!

5 You work for Lunar Landings Ltd, the first travel agency offering holidays on the moon! Your company has built a five-star resort – Moondome – which offers traditional holiday attractions as well as plenty of space fun!

Your job is to write a publicity leaflet that:

- **describes** the Moon and Moondome;
- **explains** what it is like to take a holiday in one-fifth gravity;
- **informs** people about all the things they can do at Moondome;
- **persuades** holidaymakers to give it a try!

Of course, promotional leaflets often contain pictures and maps. But remember: **don't waste time drawing** anything for your leaflet. Just mark out a box and make a quick note of what kind of illustration you would put in it.

6 Here is some information from a history book on the Tudors, about an important event in 1545:

Enemy ships from France appeared in the English Channel. The *Mary Rose* sailed out from Portsmouth Harbour, ready to do battle. It was her first voyage after being fully refurbished. Everyone on shore was confident that this beautiful ship – the pride of the fleet, and the king's favourite – could easily beat the French. Excitedly, the king and his courtiers watched from Spithead.

But the battle had barely begun when, suddenly, the great warship heeled over. As she leaned, her guns broke loose and fell into the sea. Her masts broke and her sails and rigging tore. In just a few minutes she turned on her side and sank, in full view of the shore. Seven hundred sailors were drowned. Only forty lives were saved.

Now imagine that you are a lord or lady in the court of King Henry VIII. You were with the king today as the tragedy unfolded, and now you are writing a detailed eyewitness account.

The personal journal of ....

July 19th 1545

For me, this sad day began when the palace servants woke me for an early breakfast...

7 Think of a subject you know a lot about. The challenge is to write a formal information text about this subject... but to make it so interesting and detailed that your readers will be hooked too!

Include all the interesting details you can think of. You will probably have to explain some things about your subject as well as giving straightforward information. You could include some instructions, some advice – or even some persuasion!